Self-Respect Sunday for Your Soul

. . . If You Love an Addict

A Weekly Journal

Praise for

Self-Respect Sunday with Candace

Your Self-Respect Sundays have been a gift to me for many years. I'm always so glad to get them each week because they remind me of how important it is for me to develop my own self-respect. I'm working hard to not enable the addict in my life. It's hard, but your weekly wisdom helps me stay on track. Thank you so much for that! ~ Rebecca J., Texas

Every Sunday I read your Self-Respect Sunday pieces and I find them super thought-provoking. I feel encouraged to stay on the path I've chosen, to no longer give money to my addicted daughter and to stop doing things for her that she can do for herself. Sometimes she still gets mad at me when I say no to her and sometimes I still cave in to her demands. But I feel a lot better about myself now, so it's worth it and I feel like I'm on the right track. ~ Deb K., Australia

I've been feeling very isolated because of the addict I love and the chaos he keeps causing in my life. I love him but I'm also learning how to love myself, and the Self-Respect Sundays that I get each week help me feel like someone (Candace) actually understands me, so I don't feel so alone in all of this. Thank you for all of your wonderful guidance every week. ~ Janet D., Calgary, Canada

While I feel I have made great gains in nurturing self-respect and setting boundaries, the Self-Respect Sundays remind me that this inner work is an ongoing journey of self-awareness and self-care.
~ Mona B., Vancouver, Canada

Copyright © 2021 by Candace Plattor

All rights reserved. The use of any part of this publication reproduced, transmitted in any form or by any means, electronic, mechanical, photocopying, recording, or otherwise, or stored in a retrieval system, without the prior written consent of the author and publisher is an infringement of the copyright law.

Library and Archives Canada

SELF-RESPECT SUNDAY FOR YOUR SOUL
. . . IF YOU LOVE AN ADDICT

A WEEKLY JOURNAL

CANDACE PLATTOR, M.A.

ISBN 978-0-9953162-3-2 (softcover)
ISBN 978-0-9953162-4-9 (ebook)

Published by
Candace Plattor, M.A.
604-677-5876
Candace@LoveWithBoundaries.com
LoveWithBoundaries.com

Cover and journal page designs by Linda Parke ravenbookdesign.com
Image page designs by Carole Audet

Images sourced from Pixabay and Unsplash.

Dedication

I want to dedicate this book to all of the amazingly courageous families who have come to me for help over the years—you know who you are!

When there is addiction in a family, everyone struggles—everyone suffers. Often, these families remain silent about their situation for a very long time before finally reaching out for help. That's usually when I hear from them—when they are at the end of their rope and feel like they just can't put up with it anymore. They connect with me and my Counselling Team because they want answers—even though most initially come because they need to know what they can do to "fix" the addict in their lives.

But as we continue to work together, these wonderful loved ones begin to understand that until *they* change some of the things *they've* been doing, the addicts they love so dearly won't change either. This is when their true courage emerges and the real work begins. And it's also when the ripple effects of their efforts show the difference between what is ***helping*** and what has been ***enabling***.

Thank you to all of you, who have shown yourselves to me in such deep and meaningful ways. I know you have learned from me—but I wonder if you know how much I've also learned from you. You will always be in my heart.

Candace

Acknowledgments

First, I want to thank my team of wonderful therapists and trainees—Anna, Serena, Zander, Caitlin and Misha as of this writing—for making my professional life more exciting and less lonely. Having been a solopreneur for many years basically working by myself, it has been wonderful to make the leap into putting together a Counselling Team of very talented and highly skilled associates to not only share and expand the number of families we could assist at one time, but also to keep me on my toes!

Zander Townend—who quadruples as my business coach, technical whiz kid, Addictions Counsellor on the Team, and my friend—has helped this grounded Taurus to fly a little, to think outside the box, and to even use a dreaded spreadsheet from time to time. I thank you for your astute and ongoing vision for our Team.

Carole Audet and Tracey Ehman—my Digital Content Manager and Social Media genius, respectively, who have both been with me for 10+ years. They are my right and left arms, and they each take care of many of the tasks that I will probably never be very good at. And Diane Chaisson—my bookkeeper extraordinaire, who is always there to help when the numbers drive me crazy!

To my dear friends Debbi, Tania, and Vindy—you are the sisters I never had. Thank you for your ongoing love, encouragement, and support.

My deep thanks to all of you, for the many gifts you each bring to me and to our amazing Team.

When Addiction Affects Families

I have been working with the families and other loved ones of people struggling with addiction for over three decades—and I have learned a lot. My most significant learning over these years is that when there is addiction in a family—or in any relationship—everyone is affected and everyone suffers.

My other major understanding is that, although there is a lot of help for those who are addicted—such as detoxes, residential treatment centers, outpatient addiction counselling agencies, books, and support groups—there is very little help for those who love them. And of course, the irony is that for every one addict, there are usually ten to twenty other people who are negatively affected by that one person's addictive behaviors. Proportionately, the lack of skilled and truly helpful assistance for these loved ones is a situation that desperately needs to be remedied.

When we love an addict, life is hard. We care so much about them, and it breaks our hearts to see them go through their many anxieties and tribulations. We don't understand why they keep shooting themselves in the foot with their own self-destructive choices. Sometimes, in our need to shield ourselves from the horrific damage the addict's addiction causes, we become codependent people-pleasers—which basically means that we put their needs ahead of our own on a fairly consistent basis. Our self-care and our self-respect begin to suffer as our healthy boundaries become non-existent. We don't recognize, or like, who we're becoming. And we often don't talk about what's happening in our lives for fear that others will not understand and will ultimately judge us. As a result, we don't appreciate how many, many other families are also experiencing the very same traumas we are.

How to Use This Book

Several years ago, I began sending the people on my email list a weekly piece called "Self-Respect Sunday with Candace"—a visual newsletter with quotes from my book **Loving an Addict, Loving Yourself: The Top 10 Survival Tips for Loving Someone with an Addiction**. I heard so much praise and thanks from those receiving these that I decided to put together a journal along those same lines. Welcome to **"Self-Respect Sunday for Your Soul . . . If You Love an Addict: A Weekly Journal"**—this has been a labor of love from me to you.

If you are the loved one of someone with an addiction, **this book is to help you understand yourself more deeply**. You can use it in several different ways—you can enjoy the beautiful photographs as meditative and reflective points for yourself. You can open the book wherever you like to read a quote and breathe it deeply into your experience. You can use the journal pages to write about the feelings these quotes bring up, to reflect and to set new goals for yourself and boundaries for others. Or—you can combine all of these in any way you like.

And for those of you who prefer to write a little more, I've added some extra journal pages in the back.

This book is intended as a form of self-care, to help you gently push beyond your limits and raise the bar for yourself. Mostly, it is for your enjoyment and continued self-learning. Please use this journal in whatever ways that fit for you.

All my best to all of you,
Candace

We live on a planet of free will, and we are all making choices in every moment of our lives.

Changing codependent behaviors requires courage and determination. As you begin to experience the enhanced self-respect from making healthier choices, you'll be more prepared to do what it takes to feel better about yourself and your life.

Self-respect is the most important thing we either have or don't have. When we love an addict, without inner work our self-respect is fleeting at best.

Enmeshment with an addict decreases our self-respect. You'll know you're "addicted to the addict's addiction" by determining where you are on this simple gauge:

"When the addict in my life is doing okay, I'm doing okay. When the addict isn't doing okay, I'm not doing so well."

Living with the burden of a loved one's addiction may create a sense of isolation for you. Please know that you're not alone and there are people who understand exactly what you're feeling.

Having once loved a person with addictive behaviors, I have found nothing as rewarding in my journey as saying goodbye to my own codependency and experiencing the increased self-respect that liberation has brought.

Remember – you are powerless over anyone but yourself. Try as you might to make others in your life behave differently, they won't make that choice until they recognize they have something of value to lose and then become ready to make their necessary changes.

Loving an addict means sharing in the misery of addiction – until our own healing allows for a different way of life with increased self-respect.

As you begin to set more appropriate boundaries and stick to them no matter how much others may try to dissuade you, the better chance you have of shifting into the self-respecting person you were meant to be.

The more you are looking after yourself and filling yourself up in healthy ways, the more energy and positivity you will have to give to the others around you.

Self-care is definitely an "inside job" – no one else can do it for you. It truly is your job to determine what your needs are, and you are ultimately the one responsible for meeting those needs. That is how we grow our self-respect.

Loving an addict creates a whirlwind of emotions ranging from fear, frustration and hopelessness when things are at their worst – to relief, confidence and a misguided optimism when things are at their best.

Are you used to the lies, manipulation and self-absorption of the addict you love? The truth is that all of this can change, as you choose instead to treat yourself differently and develop your self-respect.

If you allow deception and manipulation to occur in your relationships, you are not requiring enough of yourself – and you and your addicted loved one will both suffer as a result.

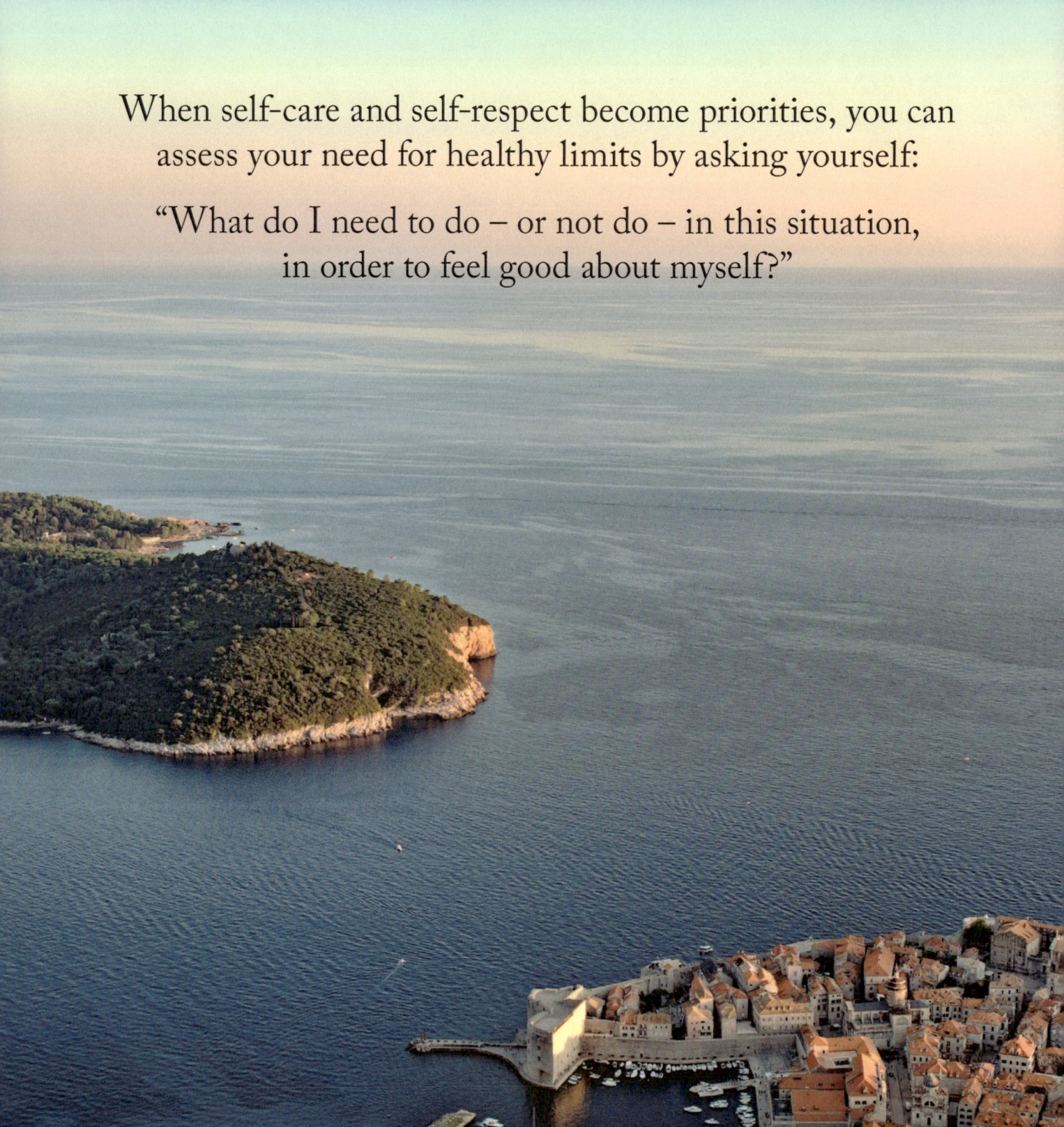

When self-care and self-respect become priorities, you can assess your need for healthy limits by asking yourself:

"What do I need to do – or not do – in this situation, in order to feel good about myself?"

We are all at choice in every single moment — and recovering from addiction is one of the most courageous choices we can make. This is precisely what is required for our self-respect to blossom.

The Self-Care Creed is:

"Although I care about other people's feelings,
the way I feel about myself is most important to me."

To be truly self-caring, you must be willing to put your own needs first when that is appropriate. Your primary concern will be about how you are feeling about *yourself* — using your healthy sense of self-respect as your gauge.

When shifting from people-pleasing to self-respect, you'll need to give yourself permission to be uncomfortable for a while as you're changing your responses toward yourself and others. Please be gentle with yourself – and enjoy the amazing ripple effects of your healthy self-care.

You need to love your addict enough to stand strong – to have clear boundaries and to let them know how their addiction is affecting you, in order to maintain your all-important self-respect.

The one person you can and should be taking care of is yourself. Holistic self-care is a wonderful gift to give yourself and is the foundation of healthy relationships with others in your life.

If you're feeling depressed, guilty or hopeless in your situation with an addicted loved one, please understand that your feelings are normal under these conditions. Self-awareness is the key – and as you continue developing your self-respect, a better life can be yours.

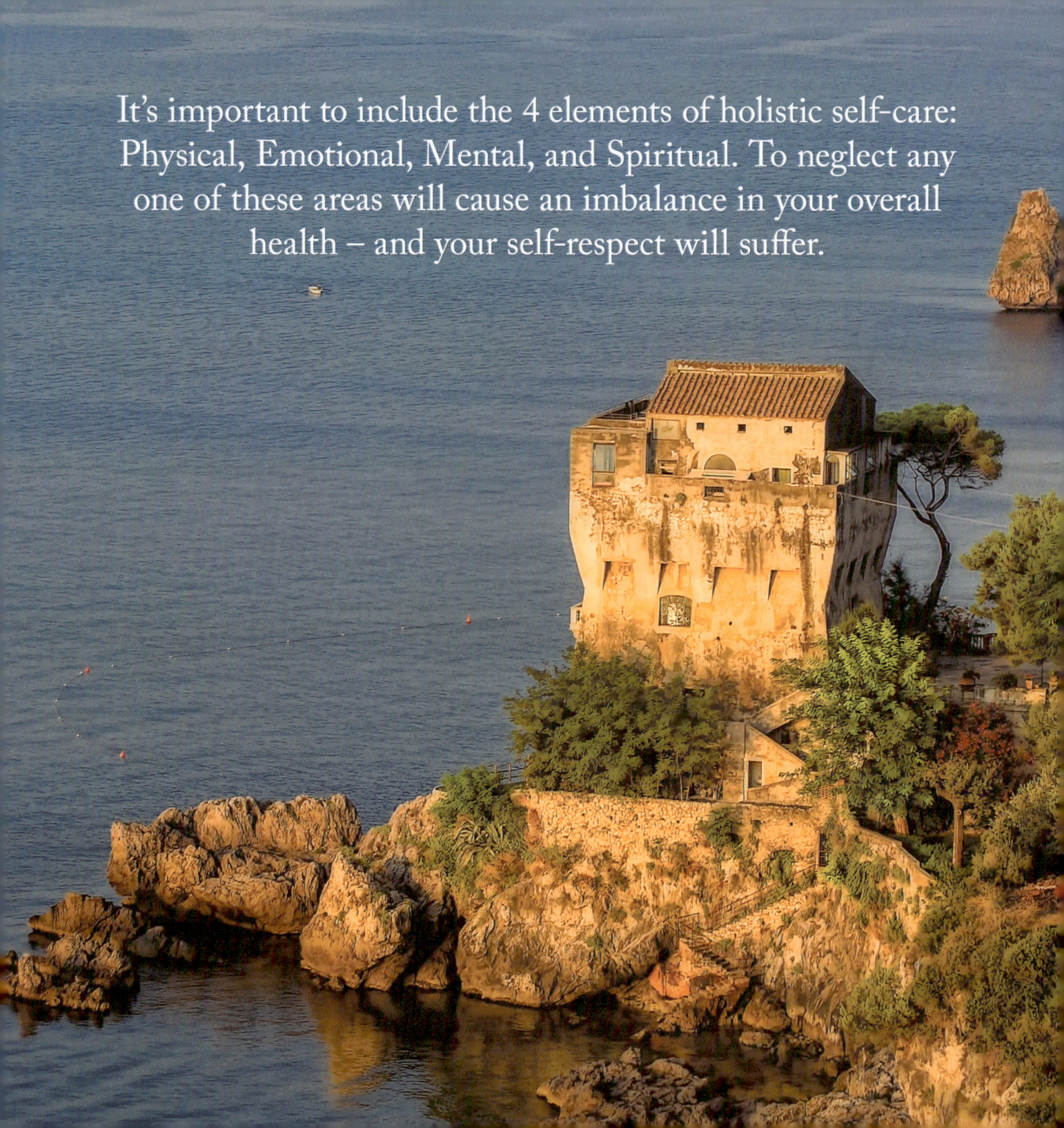

It's important to include the 4 elements of holistic self-care: Physical, Emotional, Mental, and Spiritual. To neglect any one of these areas will cause an imbalance in your overall health – and your self-respect will suffer.

My definition of codependency is a simple one:

"Codependency occurs when we put other people's needs ahead of our own on a fairly consistent basis, going to any lengths to avoid unpleasant conflict with others."

When you say *Yes* consistently to another person and when you accept any form of abuse as part of any of your relationships, you are essentially telling the other person that it's all right for them to treat you that way.

I understand that if I want my life to be different, I must be the change I want to see. Everything in my life – especially my self-respect – begins with me.

It is only when you choose to give your power and control to another person that you begin to feel the sting of codependency. It's important to understand that no one can disrespect you without your permission.

The most courageous choice you can make is to stop blaming others and instead change what you can about yourself and your life. Please remember that it's not always easy to do significant inner work, so reach out for help if you need it.

As you shift to self-respecting behaviors, you may be be surprised when other unhealthy and enmeshed relationships in your life also improve.

It's true that we teach other people how to treat us. If you are not respecting yourself, there will be others who will pick up on that and also treat you disrespectfully.

When you love an addict, you'll need to understand that *everything in your life begins with you* and ripples out from the relationship you have with yourself.

In order for the relationship with your addicted loved one to transform into something more positive, you must be willing to see how your own dysfunctional patterns may have been contributing to difficult situations. This is also how your self-respect will improve.

Here is a simple but difficult truth: if you're willing to allow an addict's self-absorbed behavior without setting self-respectful boundaries, then you really have no one to blame but yourself. Healthy boundaries increase your self-respect.

The most important work for you, as the loved one of an addict, is to build up your own self-respect. You will need to learn how to stop enabling by becoming willing to allow them to find their own way – and even hit bottom.

As you decide to practice healthier and more holistic ways of being in relationship with yourself, you will find that you are expanding your own sense of worth and value by treating yourself in ways that are more self-respectful.

One major skill you may need to learn or brush up on is setting – and maintaining – appropriate boundaries with the people in your life, addicted or otherwise, learning assertiveness techniques to help you say *No* when you mean *No*.

By deeply understanding that the addicts we love are going to make their own decisions – regardless of how hard we try to force them to do what we want – we can come off the roller-coaster of chaos and start focusing on our own lives.

Having the wisdom to know the difference between what you can and cannot change — and knowing how to change the things you can control — will create both the serenity and the self-respect that you have been wanting to find in your life.

When you start to set healthier boundaries with your addicted loved one, and take more personal responsibility for yourself and your own choices, you will soon feel more respect for yourself.

It is only when we let go of our need to change other people, and instead decide to change ourselves, that we can truly begin to heal.

Because of free will, anything that has to do with anyone other than you is not in your realm of control.

Everyone involved in relationships with an addict suffers, as typical ways of relating are replaced with one unhealthy dynamic after another. In short, life is hard – and even more difficult without the healing power of self-respect.

In order to become a healthy person physically, emotionally, mentally and spiritually, we must learn to deal with discomfort and be willing to face our life tasks even when we find them to be unpleasant.

You do not have to remain addicted to someone else's addiction. You have an open invitation to reclaim your long-forgotten needs and desires – as well as to increase your self-respect in the process.

If you love an addict, pretending that things aren't as bad as they are will not make them get better. Enabling people with addictive behaviors, as opposed to actually helping them overcome their addiction, only makes the situation worse.

For most people who care about an addict, life is full of secrets. They may not want anyone else to know, for fear of receiving judgement from them.

Because most people don't talk openly about how hard it is to love someone who has an addiction, they often have no idea of the huge number of people who are dealing with the exact same issues. There is no longer any need for shame or for silence.

If your life is in chaos because of the addict you love, it's important for you to understand that you don't have to live this way. There are alternatives to the pain you're experiencing – and cultivating your own self-respect is the most significant one.

If you are feeling a little like a doormat in any of your relationships, especially the one with the addict you love, you need to look at *what you are doing* to allow that to happen.

In every relationship it takes two to tangle but only one to untangle. Choosing to explore your own dynamics will heighten your self-respect, because your own behaviors are the only ones you have any real power to change.

In order for codependency and lack of self-respect to be part of any relationship, two things have to happen: The people-pleaser has to say *Yes* a lot more than *No*, and the other person has to not only accept this but also begin to expect that to occur. Can there be a better reason to learn how to respect yourself?

Developing self-respect is an amazing journey. As you do your inner work and begin to make different choices, you will be astonished by the wonderful rewards that await you — your entire life changes as your self-respect surges, choice by choice.

ABOUT THE AUTHOR

Candace Plattor, M.A., R.C.C. is an Addictions Therapist in private practice, where she specializes in working with the family and other loved ones of people who are struggling with addiction, in her unique and signature **Family Addiction Therapy Program**. As a former addict with over 30 years clean and sober, Candace learned that overcoming addiction is a family condition: everyone in the family is affected by addiction and everyone needs to heal. For three decades, she has been helping both addicts and their loved ones understand their dysfunctional behaviors and make healthier life choices.

The results Candace achieves have been astounding: addicts stop using and families regain their lives from the ravages of addiction. Not only has her success led to a waiting list of clients but she is also a sought-after leader in the field of addiction. As the developer of the Plattor Method of Family Addiction Therapy, Candace now works with her team of top counsellors, helping families and addicts break the cycle of addiction for good.

You can visit her website [lovewithboundaries.com] and sign up to receive Chapter 1 of her award-winning book, *Loving an Addict, Loving Yourself: The Top 10 Survival Tips for Loving Someone with an Addiction*, as well as "Like" her Facebook page [facebook.com/LovingAnAddictLovingYourself].

Be sure to check out Candace's TEDx talk titled "How to Love with Boundaries: Saying N.O.P.E. to the Addict You Love" [http://lovewithboundaries.com/tedx].

You can also see her Get Inspired Vancouver talk titled "Addiction Recovery: Empowering Addicts to Choose Not to Use" [http://lovewithboundaries.com/GetInspired].

If addiction is causing pain and suffering in your family, and you're ready to do what it takes to reclaim your sanity and serenity so you can live your best life, visit LoveWithBoundaries.com/intake-questionnaire *for a free 30-minute consultation.*

www.ingramcontent.com/pod-product-compliance
Lightning Source LLC
Chambersburg PA
CBRC090837010526
44118CB00007B/234